Ace of Hearts

The Poetic Diary of Ace Metaphor

ACE METAPHOR

CONTENTS

DEDICATION

To my mother, I love you.

To my father, I look up to you.

To my Metaphorically Speaking family, this wouldn't have been possible without you.

To my online supporters, you give me purpose – for that I am grateful.

Thank you for believing in me.

Connect with me on social media:

Facebook.com/acemetaphor

Instagram.com/acemetaphor

Send a picture of yourself holding the book to

acemetaphorpoetry@gmail.com.

Be sure to include your social media handle.

Be creative, you may be featured on one of my social media pages.

Love to you all.

This is my heart on the page.
Flowing in free verse.
No boundaries except words.
My life.
My poems.
My diary.
I wrote it all for *you*.
You know who you are.

ACE METAPHOR

MIND'S INSANE

My mind's insane
a cryptic cage of pain and rage
of detained thoughts of you
I converse
through the bars of headaches
with replays of memories of you
you are still very much a part of me
a part of me
I often hide secretly from those who
are currently interested in me
we
all
have
secrets…
mine just happens to be you…
knowing that I should just let bodies of thoughts of you
decay in a closet
instead
I imprison them in the attic
of my head
we are all victimized by words left unsaid
unsettled affairs

we have cheated ourselves out of a marriage
with the selfishness we often bed
never bared witness to him
and his awesome truth
refusing to see with the addition of him
our threefold cord wouldn't easily be broken into two
now hearts are broken in two
spinal cords are nothing more than bone and disk
no electricity exist
our love chokes in the smell of rigor mortis
we are stiff
I
the warden
you
just the collection of thoughts I miss
I keep you safe
locked deep inside the inner corridors of me
that no one knows about
there I visit you daily
during the times most people often assume
that I am daydreaming
daily
people who try to police my life
often ask about the whereabouts of you
and of course I lie
I pretend as if I don't care

I act as if in my life
you were never there
but inside I am still there
shielding the footprints we made in the sands of my heart
from the waves of father time ever erasing
I am still there
locking the cells within my cells
that hold clusters of memories of you
and your likeness
from my mind ever escaping
I am still there
making the food that feeds you
the clothes that clothe you
but hiding that fact from anyone that knows you
that
I'm just a man
obsessed with protecting pictures of you
my daily duties include making sure that they don't fade
so in a way
we can last forever
so my mind remains insane
a cryptic cage of pain and rage
of detained thoughts of you
I converse
through the bars of headaches
with replays of memories of you

you are still very much a part of me
a part of me
I often hide secretly from the women
who are currently interested in me
we
all
have
secrets...
mine just happens to be you

FREE FALL

I look over at you
as you look over at me
and once again
perfect timing
and we smile at the irony...
and the same time I reach
to grab for your hand
I realize that you're already
holding mine
and we giggle
and we close our eyes
and we count to three
then leap
into the pool uncertainty
and there is only one thing that
we are both certain of
and that is...
wherever it is
that we eventually land
that we will land *together*
because our hands are clenched together
praying that wherever we may fall

may we splash

deeply in love...

and we get our hair wet

and we soak our clothes in it

and we allow our emotions to skinny dip in it...

but in

the meanwhile

we are just enjoying the fall...

as we dive through the clouds and

somersault through the atmosphere

for our dissension

is an out of this world experience

and we experience

this experience together

so let's enjoy the fall...

let us not worry about

where it may take us

let's just

take it all in

all the sights

let us touch the horizon

let us surf all the winds

and whenever we may land

let us never forget the journey

let us never forget the laughs

and the sky

and most of all

let us hope that we *do* splash

but in the meanwhile...

let's

just

enjoy

this

fall

and make it last

SKINNY DIP

Let's rock boat unclothed
skinny dip, jump into the oceans
just to see if we float
for bodies were made to swim, jerk, dive
and ride these currents
follow this earth then see stars
for we are sea stars
I wonder if the stars can see us...
is that why they seem to always blush, wink
then twinkle at us
call for us to open up our hearts
and let the north one watch tonight
so open up the curtains to your soul
and sorta dim the lights
as skirts meet thighs
then say hi to ankles
and kiss toes goodbye
as I backstroke
behind your back, stroke
leave your body full of pleasure on one side
numb on the other
baby, it's okay to let your back *stroke*

inside your river glide, we collide

big bang then create life

we roll play Gods at night

make suns and mother natures in our image

we birth creeks when our souls' toes meet

and curl so high you can grab milky way's sheets

damn, you be having the skies so crinkly

then we drink from a cup

mortals said was way too out of our reach to touch

cause they don't know that when we fuck...

magic shit happens

I swear fairy tales come true when you do

and when you do, feel me going deeper

you swear *Pinocchio* was in you

and I was lying with every stroke

full extension with every row

deep breath with every lick

a splash with every kiss

we make waves of bliss

in this ocean

in this pool

in this creek

underneath that moonlight

beside that tree

inside this heat

this lifetime let's take ours

and be in no rush
be loud with our love
baby, no hush
let the angels hear us
I swear the heavens have never seen
explosions quite like us

COSMIC WEDDING

The candle's orange glow
races the moonlight's shine to our eyes
as we dry off into the windy nights
bodies clashing just like cannon balls
hips, splash in spaceships
we then blast off
into the horizon's seven seas
hands in clenched
deeply on this day
committed to each other before God
we take off our shirts
unbuckle our pants
and you drop to your knees
as do I
like Adam followed Eve
the naked truths of love
only covered by twigs and trees' leaves
we then plead for him to include
his heavens as our pool
his constellations as our lifeguards
we then make love...
the way leaves swimming in a whirlwind gust does

created from dust

so the distant bars on the walls of our worldly chambers

can't contain

our love's anguish unleashed

for you are my fairy tale beauty...

and although by day I am human

I am your nightly beast

and when the darkness in the sky falls

under the sheets

on you I feast

I take my father time

for you are mother nature

lightning bugs will flutter in the pits of your stomach

so illuminate as you cum

over and over again

in and out, in and out

deeper and deeper

lose your breath when I hold it there

splash into my heart with your soul

grab tight as we travel the galaxy

let go, don't fight it

be pulled by its gravity

I will forge us into one tonight

under the stars

Jupiter will be our witness

comets will halt, gather to cheer

the union created by the milky way

that bathed on Venus

we sprinkled waves of Saturn on our fingers

we now wear rings

Pluto brought them us

Mercury was your maid of honor

Orion, my best man

and Poseidon presided over the service

he preached

oceans and rivers

shakes and quivers

through slurps and jerks

we found the secret to life existing in a crevice

it read...

spitters are quitters...

and you never forfeit

so I will never give up on you

tonight

we will be wed as one

and create three

where there was previously only two

but before we do

of course I'll marry you,

I do

OCEANS

I imagine that oceans

were only granted colors

because of you

that once upon a time

Aphrodite cried her waters blue

only after learning that Poseidon

favored you

she once had his heart

until his aura was drawn to you

did you know that long ago

Gods fought over you

that the stories foretelling your birth

can be found in the dusty caves of his heaven

that there are scrolls hidden in his halls

and they call you by name

they tell of the day

an Olympian stole Zeus' thunder bolt

just so your eyes could

twinkle a little bit brighter

he saw sparks in you

so he gave you tears too

for deep down he knew

that no God could have you
that he
couldn't have you
so he whispered in your ears
that the secret to your happiness
would be found in the man
that doesn't make those tears fall
in no other moment than
the one where you say I do
and you two, too
cry an ocean blue

SO LONG

I wanna kiss you so long
your mind says so long
to those hurtful thoughts those boys left
when they did you so wrong
here now are the lips of your king
kiss them then differentiate between
what a man really is
and what a man really ain't
rub yo pretty little fingers alongside my beard
and know that I am here for the long run
or the long walk
or the long ride
or the long fly
or the long drive
or the long swim
or the long climb
or the long whichever
mode of transportation
your pretty little heart prefers
just as long you promise
to plant your soft golden hands
forever inside these palm trees mine

and feel what they feel like
know that they are of the creature
creatively created just to
rub your feet, run your bath water
and open doors for you
I told God last Tuesday
I'm ready to serve you
to lock lips with his daughter and never let go
I even purchased this shiny diamond ring
only for the outward proof
to one day show our children
that we are going to have
that that's what a real man is supposed to do
when they say "I love you"
see these boys will "say"
they will love you for a lifetime
men, however get on one knee
in front of a thousand sunsets and do right
look at me,
I'm going to do right by you
I'm going to renew my vows not every 25 years
but every night to you
then do
all those things I did to get you to fall in love with me
in the first place

even after you

cause a real man never stops earning you

or dating

or loving you

or touching you

or trusting you

or hugging you

or kissing you

or licking you

see I'ma do

all those things

over

and over

and over

stop

wiggle it little...

and start over

and over

and over again

from inside and then out

until you find the highest mountain

on the most remote part of this Earth

inside our bedroom and shout

how proud you are to call me your husband

your best friend

so when I talk about kissing you

that means now, then and until when

not even death himself can part us

cause when it's real like this is real

best believe

not even death himself

can stop us

TIME

You are proof that time doesn't exist
that it is only magically moments of us
woven carefully together by God
have you ever noticed
that since you have walked into my life,
clocks no longer tick?
so I threw them all away...
because waking up to your *good morning*
is the only alarm I will ever need
your kiss goodnight is how I know to sleep
and your heart is the most important thing
I will ever wear on my sleeve
watches
were made in your image
because you are so patient with me
so if time really did exist
it would be you...
for it is you that heals all wounds
and erodes all walls
double reinforced around hearts
for as you know
I was hurt before

and in a different dimension
alternate realities away
I remain half the man I am today
for there I didn't believe when they used to say
that *God answers all prayers in his due time*
that *all it takes to mend a broken heart is time*
because what they failed to mention is that time
would look so much like you
that it would smile the way that you do
that when you kiss time
it tocs and kisses you back
that every man
that has ever lived on the face of this Earth
only wanted more of you
time
and you could have spent yours with any man
but you choose me
for that reason I promise to cherish every second of you
for I now know
that two people don't fall in love over time
but rather the very moment
they stop believing in it
and start believe more in each other...
for I have loved you from the first time I laid eyes on you
that moment, time stood still and hasn't restarted
that's how I know that you are the one for me

real love with us

doesn't exist in hours, days or even years

it only loves in forevers

it only lives in nows

and it certainly only says I do to infinities

because you have already shown me

that our love

is and will forever be

timeless

CONCENTRATE

Some concentrate
while I debate
pulp or pulp free
I choose to live life
for its simplicity
no need for extra additives
I give her me and the simple things
like smiles and freshly squeezed hugs
love picked from the highest of orchard trees
for we are no more than mere birds
mixed with a few bees
pollen from which the purest of honey feeds
splendid but sugar free
because she is already so very sweet
and me...
I live so her flower can grow
and since love is fertilized by the air
we go wherever the wind takes us
and there
we land in a field of lions
and dandily we sprout hands
to give thanks to the soil that makes us

then we say amen...

and let God

sway our souls together

like leaves dancing in his summer breeze

and through Jesus' name

we sprinkle prayers, melodies and scriptures on his trees

with hopes that whenever the weather falls

each other we never leaf

that we only hop forward

and blossom as we spring

our love only needed the simple things

water

flavored with laughs

trust

and us

do you remember that

we once grew an enchanted forest

by simply enjoying the nature of just

us...

US

Change my number to one

only you and God knows

transform social media

until it's utterly meaningless to us

your spirit is bigger than my ring finger

so I radiate you

my aurora shouts of you

fuck it

I don't care if other girls know about you

I want them to

you are my pot of gold

rainbows

led me to you

gather the flock at the base of the mountain top

join my side and watch

as I tell the whole world about you

my fountain of youth

sprinkles and raindrops

kiss me passionately in front of the masses

I'll make love to you

I don't give a damn if they see

PHANTOM OF THE OPERATOR

Open up your windows and dim your lights low
just leave a hint of the night's shade
a bit of the moon's gray and slowly blow
baby tonight
it's okay to let your trumpets play
feel as your heartbeat gets replaced by my voice
drip wet, curl and let your soul glow in it's bass
illuminate the place
but do pace yourself
don't forget to breathe
I wanna hear each breath you take
grow a little longer with each sound make
so savor this conversation
and promise to rub slow
fill the room with the aroma of ecstasy
underneath the drummings of my congo
while you moan
I'll beat slow
just as long as you do what's told
because tonight over the phone
I'm in control
so the troubles of the world

let go

just gush

cum too

allow things to swell

faucets will run

blood will rush

baby, hush...

can you still hear me?

I am everywhere you are even if you're nowhere near me

phantom of the operator

the mask man lurking in each dark shadow of your room

can you see me dancing on your walls

like the tree's silhouettes

baby, what's the splashing?

did you say that you were wet?

can you feel me yet?

moving your curtains as I blow through your window

and when my gust creeps underneath your sheets

and it touches you on your secret parts

tingle

close your eyes and pretend it's me

tornado head

I bet you didn't know that just by using the wind

I can eat

baby rock the bed

let me hear you bang that head board

hello?

are you still there?

did I hear you say you wanted me to talk about head
more?

well okay

but before I do

I need you to do one thing for me

I need you to put down that phone

and put in your blue tooth

because tonight I need both of your hands free

take off all your rings

because tonight

I need you distraction free

then run your finger tips

up and down your canvas for me

lick one

circle the other around your nipple

began to nibble

your body is a palace of ballets

and underneath my instructions

it will sing high and low

and every note in between

baby, say my name!

say it again!

louder baby, roar!

make the type of music the neighbors can't ignore

ignite your flame

passion, verbal interaction

rave on then imagine

my wood packing your fire bed

baby, picture you are Cleopatra

and I'm giving you Egyptian head...

and our drapes are swaying

as man servants feed you grapes

dismiss them please

so I can show you how much I miss you

please, can I carry you to the pool

bring a match with you

candle light bathing off the top of pyramids

is how we spend late afternoon

sprinkle your mist on me

I'm going to take a deep breath soon

and dive further and further underwater

when you feel me press against your thighs

don't bother to resist

my tongue will be so buried deep in you mummy

giving you that King's Tut kiss

I can die now

spend eternity drowning in your pool

so relax your head

grip the sheets

arch your back

the spirits are watching

calling for you to cum more

so rewind this foreplay

for play

let's give them an encore

as you put your pillowcase over your face

and rub your prize more

then soak your satin sheets

orgasmic thoughts anytime

my words and your brain meet

so roll your eyes to the back of your head

mind fucking can you see it

can you touch it

wanna stroke it?

press play, then slow more it

tonight!

I'm going to fuck you

in all of your favorite sexual positions

over the phone

and all you have to do

is listen...

LIKE POETRY

Damn

just counting the ways to get to know how you taste

has my mouth watering so much

I'm slobbing and shit

all over this poem…

thinking about the orgasmic

the cataclysmic earth shaking shit

I'm going to do to your clit

the conversation between my lips and it

is in sense like

poetry...

the way I *spear* my tongue in

as I intensely pear into your eyes

my taste buds so deep into you

on the tip of my tongue I feel your temperature rise

as you rumble and *shake*

I call that maneuver Shakespeare

and I take pride in getting your Ju-le-wet

as my mouth Rome-in-yo

Cap-you-let

me perform monologues in that shit

like *to eat*

or not to eat

for I dare to swear

that your nectar will be the death of thy self

but I'd gladly sip and take the trip

to your ecstasy's after life

just so I can feel you get up after I pass out

and lick your juices off my lips after you cum too

for on this stage

in this play

there's absolutely no me climaxing without you

damn!

I love licking poetry into you

69 SHADES OF ACE

Me

and you

dungeons and dragons

pink peacock chains

pain

flamethrower

hurt has never felt so good

you in lace under garments and a leather choker

spiked

be sure to close the doors to my corridors tight

locked it

no escaping

tonight...

you are not in control

I am

cold clamps and fastened straps

tighten

do what's told

behold, the closet is right over there

walk to it

pick a whip

bring it to me

brace yourself

and don't you flinch

hickeys begin to trail from back to neck

gentle tease ease

wrist to pillars, I'll hook you

dim red light flickers

soundproof chambers

echos

gasping

jerking

clapping

friction

pinching

scratching

the repeated clicking of fancy contraptions

between your thighs

potions dripping

slapping

hand around hair, attaching

tape, my style cocoon wrapping

cause handcuffs ain't strong enough

I like my love tied up

you cum when I say so

blindfolds

ropes, hold

your mouth full, still muffled doe

inhale me as you breathe heat

then reactivate that dry wax

that before I poured

all over your body

lashes clashin across your back and

ecstasy

sweet stings

moans splashing

spread thin over my lap

paddle action

safe word:

there is none

first aid kit

we might need one

want a water break?

you got to earn one

fight back

bite

push

cuss

claw

scream

kick

yeah, all that

struggle to not climax

not to tap out at the apex

fail

take a hit, relapse

as bound restraints are being placed

each one sealed with a gentle kiss

machine switch, turned on

moment of silence

listen with anticipation as you hear the vibrating hiss

silver bullets, metallic taste

pleasure chest

wands, wizards and gadgets

see the wall's silhouette

see as I lay pipe, glowing

while at the same time, maneuvering the toys just right

plug everything

tools

beads, poles, and an assortment of rotating things

fingers grab, choke; just right

licks, inserted inside

saliva and cranked tongue rides

twisted torture

orgasms back to back

beg me to stop

no...

cause run away this time

you cannot

the bed has buckles

scout's honor

I know how to tie a knot

swings

wedges

broken mirrors

masks

sweat out your edges

makeup

long sleeves

and scarfs

for work the next day you are going to need

as will I...

for I command you to

hit me back as you ride

pound on me as I pound harder

don't just ask me

pull me in deeper

costumes and dark rooms

candles; medieval scent

smoke and romantic gloom

pleasure and pain bask in it

let's make love like we hate each other

use the anger bottled up

from when we frustrate each other

show me the shades of you no one get to see

and in return

I'll show you the 69 shades of me
we will bathe
pray
kiss
we will live...
at some point we will have kids
and
years down the lines
at our 40th and 65th
someone will catch the sprinkle in your eyes
and the tinkle in mine
they will ask us
how did we keep are flame going in our relationship?
we will smirk and say
it wasn't always easy...
we had to fight for it

LOVE IN OLD AGE

I wanna hold your hand in a nursing home one day
when we've grown old and wrinkled
because that type of thing will never get old to us
for our aged flesh
would become timeless when we touch
and when we'd hug
and when we'd squint at each other intensely
through bottle thick glasses
as we struggle to put our dentures in before we kiss
and drip
our calloused fingertips
in a busy tub of bengay before we rub
cause nothing will relieve muscle and joint pain
caused by arthritis like massages by me
and my old man's romance would be
gently spooning you things like already chewed food
or warm apple sauce sprinkled with your favorite heart medication
cause no matter what the nurses say
feeding you things
will always be my job

just like it's my job to bathe you everyday

so tell the aid she can take the night off

cause tonight

it's going to be a lot of bumping and slapping

cussing

and gumming

bones cracking

hips dislocating

gait belt spanking

shaking

you throwing it back

me using my favorite cane

for bracing

hearts racing

lungs, albuterol inhaling

geriatric bed breaking

call light yanking

sex making

then we embracing each other's souls when we are done

as I tongue stories of our life together

so deep in your soul for so long

you actually cum to memories

from so long ago

those nights not even alzheimer's

would make you forget my name

and there we'd lay

with your salt and pepper flavored head

cradled on my chest

growing a smile that only a women that has been licked right

by a faithful mouth

all her life could have

as you feel me began to slowly creep

my hands so deep down in your depends

cause even at 90

I promise to still be giving you booty rubs until you fall asleep

proof that there are just some things that age will never change

that with some guys

chivalry will never die

that our love is supposed to last past a lifetime

and at night, times

you'd rub your eyes before looking at mine

gather a few of the last sane thoughts you have left

to say

you better not die on me

cause that would be rude and probably make me cry

you'd remind me that

a gentlemen never makes a lady cry

fighting back tears I'd look at you and I'd reply

the only reason I have to wake up, every morning

is to not let you down

that as long as you're still alive I'll be around

so that I could hold your hand in a nursing home bed one day

when we have grown old and tired to prove

that when I said in sickness and in health

that meant rather you're walking or wheeling

talking or having trouble remembering

kisses and children

your name or mine

through tumors benign or malignant

I'd still love you the same

I'd still kiss you the same

hug you the same

I'll make love to you…..

the same

nah better, cause I bet some things

get better with time

but no matter how old or sick we get

you will always be my boo

my sweetheart, my bae

you will forever be my old ass Beyonce

so when I say

that I wanna make love to you tonight

that means well past our youth

into old age

into eternity

FATHER TIME

If I shall lose my memory one day
and forget everything there is to know about me
I only pray that some days
I am able to muster up the mental strength
to mumble remnants of your name
it wouldn't be much...
just a few simple syllables on the surface
but just enough to give you strength to
by my bedside remain
for me to remain in your heart
to fill it with the memories of us
and our life together
to remind you that together
we were and still are
something very special
those moments would be so special
to *you*
I can even picture you
and the smiles those sorta words
would bring *you*
for days then
would try to bring *you*

so many frowns

so many moments filled with a life

of ours

turned upside down

but I know right now

that no matter how hard it would get

you would never stop *trying*

I can see you

trying

to hold our family together, while

trying

to take care of me

the bills

the kids

the house

all

at the same time

then finding time *trying* not to cry

at those two jobs

you would have to work

full time

just to halfway

make ends meet

in the corner *trying* to meet

a small fragment of time

with yourself

so you can just sit
for one moment
and rest...
without being interrupted by me
trying to drive to a job
I used to have
cause in my mind I would be so confused
you will have hidden the keys
more times than you can count
trying to keep me safe
marriage wasn't supposed to be this hard and *trying*
but it would be...
and I know
you'd be doing such a good job
at it
for us...
so if I shall lose my memory one day
I only pray that some days
I am able to muster up the mental strength
just to mumble remnants of your name
I know it wouldn't be much...
just a few simple syllables on the surface
but just enough to remind you
that you are still on my mind, you
are forever in my heart, that you
in a brain filled with empty space

and lost memories,
would be the only thoughts worth thinking for
so even though it would be tough
and at times
I know you'd feel like giving up
those moments you'd know
that I am on the inside
fighting father alzheimers
not to forget you
that I'm *trying* too
just as hard as you
but it's not my fault
I'm losing...

PAST 12

I wanna adorn you with a fancy dress
made from everything money can't buy
seam it with dreams
a dash of glitter
a pinch of smiles
and a handful of sparkly things
baby...
do you wear high heels
or are glass slippers more your thing?
are horse drawn carriages
more your style?
do you remember the last time
someone made you feel like you were still
a princess past twelve
or has it been awhile?
take this carpet ride with me...
let's surf the windy nights
in search of life
love
let's be free
with you in that dress
on this day
in this time
having a dance with me

DANCE WITH MY DAUGHTER

8 months ago your mother told to me
that we would be expecting you
now here you are
our little princess
addressed from the Gods
God dressed you in gold
for he knows that one day
the world will come to know you as Queen
being destined to be
greater than we
always demand to be treated as such
for look you already have your crown
and if anyone ever asks to see it
bat those adorable eyes of yours
snap then sass, say
my daddy says it's found inside my heart
smile and brighten their day with that sunshine
just like you brighten mine
know that I've prepared all my life
to protect your rays
to raise you right
your mother raised you right from her belly

and placed you right inside these arms

know, that as long as you are inside these arms

nothing will ever be able to harm you here

for your daddy's here to guard you

until that heartbeat you hear

right now in your ear

drumming and thumping stops pumping

then restarts

because I'd go toe to toe with death

just to see you grow

it feels like death

just to hear you cry

I cry too when you do

it hurts to even think about

something

someone

or some boy

ever hurting you or mistreating you

promise me that the next man

you will ever let hold you this close

will be one that loves you as much as I do

that dips when you do

catches, then props you back up

spins you in his love like I do

I've been waiting all my life

to have this dance with you

your first here
right here
in the middle of this hospital to prove
that when a man is truly right for you
he will take every opportunity he has
to dance with you
no matter where or who's looking
just like I do
but until then and even after when
I will be there for you every dance step of the way
from school first days
to good or bad first dates
my heart will be there to dance you through it
so place your hand right here on my chest
during the times life tries to beg you to quit
just rock right
put your little feet upon mine
anytime you don't remember the steps
then let's take two to the left
for boys will come and go
and sometimes make cry
the world and disney will try
to make you think that your happily ever after
begins with *him*
but I'd wipe every tear
from those eyes every time

dip you

sip you

show you

thats your happiness starts within the inside of you

you will always be enough for you

man or not

you will forever be a Queen

king or not

so let's rock and do this dance

over

and over again

for the rest of life

cause it's me

you

your beautiful mother…

until death do us part

and then some...

DAUGHTER OF THE SUNDANCE

You are made from the sugar cane

of the lands your foremothers used to bathe

therefore claim their beauty as your birthright

for isn't your last name

daughter of the sundance?

so strike a pose

hold your head high with pride

flash

your pearly whites

then show this world that there is such a thing

as African ballerina

but as you smile a while for the cameras

stay focused

for there are some in this room that will laugh if you fall

they do not want you to succeed

they have called everything

natural about you ugly

but daughter please do not believe

for remember young lioness

that your very heartbeat is the product

of the thunderous tribal calls

you are far too young to recall

so as the poachers' insults fly

and you feel yourself on the brink of succumbing

to their false standard of beauty

don't

just dance

gifted child

cry aloud

then allow your ancestors' spirits to surround you

for they will pray upon you a great gust

from the smoke fires of their ancient wooden huts

and when that dashiki wind

wraps around your skin

wear it

so that you too may pirouette in its current

for haven't your heard

a great storm on your natural hair is coming

so find the tallest African tree

buried in the ghetto of your foreign country

proudly embrace its shade

for the forecast calls for rain

and it will not let up

so when it showers

and your luscious hair starts to curl

refuse to allow the humidity of humanity to call them naps

pat your hair with confidence daughter

moisture is not your enemy

humbly remind them that you are just beautify black

for they will try to use that fact

to humiliate you

and further alienate you from

the true meaning of black beauty

so don't look outside your blinds

without grabbing your rifle of righteousness

for you will find a mob standing

chanting for you to come out the house

looking less like betty shabazz

and more like a *bad ass bitch*

but don't listen

for bitches were not made in the wonderful image of God

black queen you were

weren't you given the same texture of hair

that the son of God wore?

therefore your hair couldn't possibly be a curse

from God

but rather a reward

and anyone forming a weapon against what he created perfect

is subject to a holy war

but as you sound the war drums

prepare your heart

because when the cloudy haze over the crowd starts to fade

you will be able to make out their faces

you will see that the ones in the crowd

that will make fun of you the most

and laugh at you the most

will be other women

whose skin is of the same pigment

and they

will try to teach you to hate yourself

they will say

you were only given hips and ass

to shake, twerk and gyrate

that you are exactly the way rap music paints you to be

but tell them no they are mistaken

that you were given those hips and that ass

to bear the greatest generation

filled with the greatest warriors

and they will all wear the natural hair of kings and queens

so wear your black color proud young princess

your hair is crown

take your bow

daughter of the sunshine

spin, close hips when

they try to convince you that your hair

is too curly

that it needs to be straight

stomp

shout no!

then arabesque for it's already blessed

with an extra kiss of melatonin

so

plie

daughter

plie

for one day

your king

will hold each side of the landscape of your face

and upon the horizon of your forehead

he will plant a kiss

you will grow a smile

as you feel him caress his hands

through the texture of your natural hair

then you will know that he doesn't care

how long it is or how straight it is

only that it is his alone

then he will thank God for that backside

not for how fat it is

but because it will support you

as you sit upon your black throne

daughter of the sundance

so strike your pose

hold your head high with pride
show them that there is such a thing
as a beautiful African ballerina
but…
before you can convince *them* of this
you must first convince yourself
that you are already beautiful
the way God made you

BEFORE OUR LOVE

Thinking that today was posed to be our day

just as I watch this day slowly pass

and the opportunity for us

fastly fade

waiting

love does for no one

but yet

I still wait for her

hurrying back

knowing that she is not

not knowing if she's hurt

or if she's just hurting me

cause every second is like a stake implanted in my core

every minute going deeper and deeper

reminding me of her missing presence

proving false that outta sight is

not really outta mind

cuz she's on mind more

when she's outta sight

but it's like

even when she's gone

I still see her

somewhere inside me

what a wonderful insight

because before her

my inner world proved to be formless

and there was nothing but darkness

formed around it

that is

before a bond was created between me and her

then there came to be light

land emerged from the watery depths of our souls

giving us both ground to stand on

and upon our relationship's conception

there born a division between her day and my night

I'm darkest without her

and her light.

but dark skies fill with stars of my memory of her

illuminates it just fine

until the return of her sun in the morning time

and to the return of our son

love

which we made in our image

in the evening time

even the times

you leave

you leave a part of you with me

and even though it hurts when you're gone

it's never long

before you come home

so I'll be waiting

BEFORE THE SANDS

I rebuild cities in my mind and we still live, *there*
our small cottage home still sits on fifth and ave
exactly where you would remember it to be
and the corners of it
still smells
of pink lavender
a warm slice of apple pie
still sits
on the counter
and the sink to the right of it
still leaks
no,
I have yet to find the time to repair it
yes,
that bouquet of flowers
I used to apologize for that said lack of time
is still abloom
and our room
is still so messy
but for good reason...
mind blowing make up sex
being that reason
no,
we didn't make our bed afterwards,

did we ever?
no,
because together we decided that
getting up
just to make it
only to lay right back in it again
would be weird
and we were not weird
see there
our bed stays unmade...
everything in our home
is perfectly the way
we left them
unweird
just like we like it
and everyday after work
I rush home
sit in *our* driveway
peek through *our* window
and see you
doing nothing more than just being
there
standing in the kitchen
whistling
looking all cute just *existing* and shit
pans
sizzling
mmmmm

making brussel sprouts and chicken
our favorite dish
grinning
still seasoning that chicken
so you never find the time
to empty hangers
in this world
your clothes are still in our closet
there
we never become strangers
we are far too busy
doing the things
we once took for granted
like *being and existing*
to leave
and I am too occupied with *eating your delicious chicken*
to ever lie
like I did
my mouth
is too full with that world's truth
so there we are
chewing on chicken
sipping wine
sitting on a bed that's still unmade
catching our breathe
after just having had amazing make up sex
in a world where we still believe in
making

up…
there is only laugher
absolutely
no
crying
no pain
no cheating
it's against the rules there
there
it's so much better
than the world we now live in
for I don't know where you are anymore
or even if you
are still *being or existing*
for when the dust settles
after that sandstorm,
what's still standing
I imagine things are no longer
the way we left it
it's impossible
incomprehensible
that so much force can ravage
something so delicate
and it not be in pieces
I know you have left me...
but I'm too afraid to open my eyes to see
so I remain buried
in the sand

in the remains
and there I pretend
that things are the way
they used to be
that our house is right there
standing *still*
and we are in it
living
just being *still*
like we were
before the sands
before the winds
before the cheating
before the fighting
before the lying
before I failed you
and I
and I can't accept it
so I am
still in the debris
dreaming of that world
where I
achieve my atonement
find my redemption
a world where
I saved you
a world where
I never lose my grip

a world where
my fingers never start to slip
a world where
our love is still alive
and we
are
there
together in that world
eating chicken
sipping wine
giggling
and things are exactly the way
we left them
messy
just like we like them
a world where I can still
park in our driveway
and see you *still...*
in the kitchen, grinning
doing nothing more than just *being*
the way you were
before the sands
before winds
before you packed up
and before you were his
so my mind remains insane...

RELATIONSHIP GRAVEYARD

We loved in a fist of anger
knuckle punch holes into walls
to match the dark ones
slowly growing in our hearts
we only kissed
because our lips taste of venom
and long ago we threw the antidote away
when we said I do
I always wondered why our families
wore black to the wedding
maybe they knew
that this wasn't the going to be
the best day of our lives
but rather the funeral
they gathered
to watch us box ourselves in
this body shaped hole
under the altar
as we exchanged rings
we covered ourselves with soil
I think we thought love would grow
but rage...

rage could always fertilize tombstones
they sprouted after every Sunday service
one said I love you
others fuck you
most said I hate you
these stone cold messages
filled the lands of our text threads
so much so
they resembled over capacitated cemeteries
our bedrooms we filled with flowers
after every argument
but our romance smelled less like ecstasy
and more like a decorated graveyard
we are mere broken mirrors of ourselves
and you cut me
every time I try to reach for your heart
but I don't bleed
cause when the moonlight shines through
we emerge as zombies
mindlessly walking through this relationship
when hungry
we eat each other's sanity for breakfast
you haven't bought new clothes
since we were resurrected
when we cuddle
you say you can't hear my heartbeat

that's because it's no longer there

and I haven't touched you in ages

I imagine you have cobwebs growing down there

your favorite toy you named Charlotte

our yard is

eerie mist filled

with trees whose fingers dance on the neighbor's kid's
wall

coupled with our screams

he ain't slept in ages

and I can't feel anything

anymore

to say that I am unhealthy

is an understatement

so I just want to know

is this what happens

to till death do us part

when two people already died inside of the relationship

because I just want to love more than life itself again

but how can I

when I'm with you

and when I'm with you

I feel as if

I can no longer live

LOVE'S ABYSS

You love the twisted torture

don't you

admit it...

you couldn't leave me alone if you wanted to

you are too addicted to this sorta *romantic pain*

the spinning

the loose carousels

you're dizzy

and I think you like it...

do you even know what you are holding on for anymore

is it the hope of finding the better you need

does that fuel you

the deceit

flows through your atoms

so Eve

are you sure you're not just loving in vain...

cause your head's spinning...

who else is going to love me

listen to the things you say...

ask yourself

are you *Abel* to give selflessly

or are you still handicapped from loving a Cain

cause God is not here

so outside of his garden we stand

not holding hands

naked

we are far from paradise now

but what lessons did we gain

heartache

lies

cheating

is that what we were placed on this earth for

because we search for happiness everyday

but we are only finding war

and we don't even know what we are fighting for

cause if it ain't to have children

what are we laying for

are we just lying for

the lion or

do we need to be honest more

and admit to our treason

too afraid to be lonely

is that the reason

bodies are deceiving

so the same bed we sleep in

as we are feeding

constantly on what we

are feening

the self destruction

from loving each other

suicide bombers

explosives wired tight to our chests

and all we do is hug each other

while insides are blown to pieces

I love you to pieces

in your hands, are pieces of me

this can't be healthy

how much you mean to me

I mean

how often you are mean to me

we say *I'm sorry*

way more then we say *I love you*

to one another

cause we love the twisted torture

the spinning

the loose carousels

as long as we got each other

spinning

we don't care if it's hell

lovin the shit we been in

don't care if it smells

the scent of sulfur

the darkness we long for

welcome to love's abyss

where the worst I treat you

the deeper you fall for me

but I need you here

so stay alive

just

breathe

sEX

When I have sex with her
I pretend she's *you*
but luckily
she loves to role play
and she secretly plays *your* part well
and I dim the lights on our act
cause in the dark
well...
I would sorta say she favors *you*
she even moans the ways *you* do
and when I put my bone
so deep in her
my spirit pierces her bones
her body whispers to me
the deepest secrets
unlocked from her marrow
but my ears hear them
told to me in *your* voice...
for in the closets of my mind
I'm still stuck fucking *your* skeletons
I don't fuck her like I miss her
I fuck her like my calls missed *you*

like the only reason I land in her bed

is because *you*

didn't pick up

so I pick her up

lick her neck

down

around

and up

just to see

if she

tastes of *you*

if she shakes like *you*

she do

she cums even

to the same tricks

you do

she looks

so

much

like

you

same lips

same hips

you both have the same frame

so much in common

sisters is how you could be related

which is ironic

cause when I ask her who her daddy is

she closes her eyes

and also screams my name

so I make love to her repeatedly

because when I close my eyes

I can picture *you* are calling me

and I always cum to *you*

and for those few orgasmic moments

things between us are perfect

in her

our souls link hands and dance

to the rhythm of her moaning

and we

imagine that percussion

is timeless laughs we had over breakfast in the morning

and things are the way they used to be

like the days when we first fell in love

you and me

so with her, yes

I pretend

so I can relive our first dates

during her foreplay

I even give her key kisses down low

cause it reminds me of the high

we had when we first locked lips

making possible for me to live out
our whole relationship between her hips
so I fuck slow…
for each stroke
is a chance for us to be
again
for me to hold *you* again
the *you*
you used to be
yes...
you still occupy the same body
so sex with *you* still feels sorta the same
but *you* are far from the woman I used to love
and that currently shares my last name
so in my insane mind
I choose to have sex with that woman
and I pretend she's *you*...
so to answer your question…
yes
I am cheating on *you*
but not with any other women
I'm cheating on *you*
with *you*
woman *you* used to be

OR IS

Drawing to an end

this good thing is

is loving what's ending

a good thing

and is not seeing the big picture

a small thing

or is

that the reason you're leaving

is me leaving the past behind

being too blind

ignoring your signs

the reason why I can't figure out where your heart is

or is

it that my heart is that in which it is hiding

is my love what's blinding

is that the reason I can't see what the truth is

or is it so

that there is really no

truth

no deeper meaning in your actions

no need for interpretation

is it so

that the extent of your love speaks for itself

is what it says

what I'm hearing now

nothing

or is

DOES AN IT MAKE A SOUND?

If a heart breaks
in the middle of a lonely chest
and there's no one around
to hear it
does it make a sound
I know
but I suspect
you don't...
cause when our tree hit the ground
you were nowhere around to be found
only I was there left to quiet the cries
and the sounds were deafening
and I found in the debris
no previous signs of a collapse
so this has me questioning...
how when the tree of our love fell
was your heart
laps away
you must have had a warning
and pulled away
you didn't think of warning me
you couldn't have thought of me

cause I stayed in that forest

trying to save an already abandoned tree

answer me this...

when you didn't see me escaping behind you

you didn't think

about me

you just *left me*

so here

in a wilderness I once call ours

standing by the branches

that once held our home

I am

wondering

pondering

asking

if a man cries

at the side of an abandoned

tree

and no one's around to hear him

does his heart make sound

IN HER GARDEN

I was made from her rib
crafted in the soils of her garden
there…
it took me just six days to find myself complete
on the seventh
her heart found me and we
rested until the eighth's eve
and she became my Eve
even the angels were envious and jealous
because she
was so angelic
scoped from the image of God
her beauty was that of Eden
her fruits were for seeing *not eating*
they were like my *Adam's apples*
for every evening
words I spoke spat little seeds of her proof
that every *atom* of our existence
was created to love one another
she became was my evidence
of every naked truth unseen
and we remained unclothed

in that young garden
for it was a sin to mask her beauty
for to the world it was to be seen
and until that point of time
a voice so siren
so sweet
had went unheard
until her lips unleashed a herd
a stampede of raw emotions
streamed with ringing bells
whistles
and tambourines
every time she called my name
every night afterwards
we slept clinched in each other's perfect arms
cradled in the bosom of paradise
I remember on one particular night
in my mind's unconscious eye
I climb a mountain so high
and there I receive my life's instructions
my reason for being a being
and
my reason for being a being
was being a being for her
and *being* fruitful with her

subduing the world with her kind

filling the earth with her sunshine

and sunrays

for some days the sun didn't rise

until her eyes rose

and we chose

to speak a language

they later called love

and in it

we talked so fluently

and that language

they later called love

was to be taught to our kids

and their kids'

kids would tell their kids

of the seventh day

when mommy saved daddy

and of God's glory

cause *gawd*

just seeing her body gave glory to God

it just had to be God that crafted her garden

for her eyes were those of daisies

her chest

was a land of milk and honey

her body was a promised land

I promise

there were rivers to the east

mountains to west

and in the middle of her chest

where her heart is

stood a tall tree

and on that tree grew forbidden fruit

which she told to me

no man was to eat

for the very day of you eating from this tree,

our love would die

but somewhere

somehow

along the way

from that day to this day

a snake of deceit

told me

something different

now I'm outside her garden

wondering why those forbidden fruit

I had to eat

why in her garden

did I have to cheat

I guess

we are only to our Eves

what we eat…
I was given paradise
and ate my perfect blessing away
I urge you to
watch what you eat
for what you eat could leave you too
Eve-less

MAN, WOMAN AND TREE

If I could dim the celestial lights
mounted in the cathedrals of evil
so your endorphins would release
a muteness upheaval
leading to the stained glass windows
of your soul shattering
so that its shards of happiness
could puncture its proof
I would
to prove to you
that I am as real as love
that my heart is a clock docked
in the middle of a moving pulpit
timeless ticking with its second hand wishing
for your love resurrection
for your hands
have lathered the Lazarus
residing inside the side of my wrist
my pen passed for three days without you
your ghost showed up in spirit shortly thereafter
you are hope of a better day

in the pews of my clouded life of misdirection and confusion

you are the ray

you are the sunshine for righteousness

in the my moon influenced lunar ways

together we create gravity

not professing to your effect on the tides of my soul

simply would be blasphemy

I imagine when God created Adam and Eve

he had to be thinking of you and me

because we, were his manifestation of the phrase

made for each other

the punity of perfection

but now just like biblical martyrs

we live as constant examples of what happens

when he leaves the fruits of his labor in man's hands

we devoured our promise

and tried to move on without him

but sin's juices are still branded on our hands

so now we never use our hands when we pray

nor do you ever say amen

cause you have lost your trust in them

I being the main reason

confessions sit on the tips of our tongues

but release to them

by either one of us is done

therefore I am thoroughly convinced
that life is at its core
man, woman and tree
that happiness can only be achieved
when there is harmony between all three...

ONLY IF SHE KNEW

I wonder whether she ever knew
that every breath formed around my tongue
to formulate a word
to her
was true
because I'm beginning to think
those deep expressions of internal feelings
symbolized through words were
exactly that
just words to her
getting to her
was like moving unmovable mountains
but only if she knew
that if she put the faith of mere mustard seeds
in these seeds of words
we could transplant those mountains
break all those barriers
and bury her problems away
and we
meaning me and her
would grow along with those seeds
and every day would be

peaceful and greater

and we

would just kick back

and enjoy the fruits of our labor

but that's only if she knew...

cause it seems to me

the only thing she knows

is walking away

and I can't say I don't understand why

for even roses grow thorns

to protect themselves

and my beautiful rose had a hard time sprouting up

so thorns sprouted up

so quickly

false dreams of streams of sunshine

remove her innocence

so quickly

a quick tongue lashing against her

like winds

became the reason for her defense system

but only if she knew

that in my eyes

there has never been rose petals as blue as hers

and even though it hurts holding on sometimes

because of the thorns of hers

care

joy

happiness

love

to my hand would in time be my glove

but that's only if she knew

and deep down

I know she really does

she just doesn't show it

LOVE-LON THE GREAT

Unguarded walls is how the fire started
blaming me is what fed the flame
of its undying hungry
its rage filled rampage grows by the day
my heart's no longer safe
the land of our love
used to be such a beautiful place
it's unrecognizable now...
I can hardly see its face
rumbles shake the foundation
it's dying heart's pace
do you hear the city's cries
within the lies
that bound our efforts to save our sacred place
within the lines
lie deeper meanings that we refuse to cross
saving ourselves from the engulfing flame
but at what cost
look at what's lost
see what's stolen
thieves take refuge in the house
that once castled our future

deception now lies in between the sheets of our minds

conceiving a life that brings ruin to mine

a seed that grows fruits of regret

weeds that strangle from its roots

progress steps

the kingdom is fallen slowly

my soul is forced to watch

the memories of our city

screaming

crying

hoping

dying

my soul is forced to see

dreams of our city

sighing

lying in pain

burning alive

and I watch from the door steps of our crumbling promises

time's hands stopping

only to crush what our

blood

sweat

and tears took time to build

paralyzed

I am unable to revive what our

blood

sweat

and tears took time to kill

still

I remain alive

within the corridors of our abandoned castle

carving into its walls the stories

of its rich history

preserving its timeless mysteries

recording for all to see

that once upon a time on this desolate waste land that's sure to follow

stood a great city

that me and you built

LEFT HANGING

My eyes open

I am unfamiliar with my surroundings

vision still cloudy

my hands are bound behind me

I can't break free

where am I

who are they

those strange faces of hate

there are fires ablaze

is that a branch above me

rope around my neck

struggle to break free

over

and repeat

no, its grip and hold on my throat only get tighter

the crowd cheers

the harder I try

the floor drops beneath me

the forest erupts

my throat collapses

my mind is racing

I can only think of you

I soon find ease in my fading consciousness
with thoughts of you
blank stares
filled only with the longing to see you
once again
blacking out...
blacking out...
goodb...
wait...
who's that
I see
there
in the center of the crowd
it's you
help me!
help...
help!
why aren't you helping!
hold on
you're grinning
why
is that gold you're counting
it is...
blacking out
blacking out
no!

no!

no!

it all makes sense

it all seems so clear

it

was

you!

wasn't it

you the reason I am here

aren't you

you son of a bitch!

all the time

I was soul searching

self blaming

to try to figure out the reason for

my suffering

my pain

losing myself

being lost

led astray

trying to find your heart

it

was

you!

all along

you!

you were that one that hurt me
you were that one that betrayed me
you were that one that set me up
it
was
you
wasn't it
you were the one
that left me...
hanging

TIRED

I get that you're tired...
I'm tired too
so tired of *literally being your tire*
I'm so tired of rolling over for you
each and every time you decide to
move on
and then come right back
like my e-*motions* are *your* vehicle
your means of transportation
you walk right in
like you own the place...
prance past the kitchen
that is not yours
and open the unlocked doors to *my heart*
turn the keys to my self esteem
ignite my core
laugh
then drive away
with my self worth
I think it helps you feel better
helps you feel needed
wanted

but in the process

you drain me

you just take your joy ride

then bring the realities of we

back to me on empty

every time

leaving me

with no sustainable amount of self confidence

in my tank

you have driven many miles on my engine here

ran my heart straight into the ground

and ran off with the last engineer

now I'm parked here

unable to start loving

again

thinking about how I could just allow you to power steer

outta my life

and leave me like this

again

so outta gear

again

in need of a new transmission

no!

not again

I'm on a new mission

this time has to be different

my heart is made in a new year

new make

and

model

now equipped with a stick

so you coming back into my life

is no longer automatic

no longer are you allowed to clutch my heart

or know its schematics

I'm sorta outta your class now...

rides now

are reserved for the more deserving

the more self serving

so I'm good

I don't need your emotional pick up anymore

my self esteem has found its own ride

HOW TO LOVE A BROKEN PERSON

Instructions...

gently place glass to mouth

open...

reluctantly taste the dry emptiness of my transparency

crunch...

it starts as a very painful sensation

a quite peculiar flavor

but swallow still...

the sharp edges will only hurt until numbness is achieved

digest...

jagged pieces will slowly become a part of you

metabolize ...

how else can we build a sand castle in your heart

if you don't?

I told you from the beginning

I was broken

and that this

is how to love a broken person...

MOMENTS

Countless moments filled
with heavy thoughts and blank stares
have now become the makeup of my days
the same smiles that used to make my days
break my days
reminiscing about the faces I'm missing
empty from the holes
missing
missing the pieces of my life that used to fill them
those missing pieces are now filled with loneliness
and it's consuming every voided piece of me
my life and its peace unavoid
there is no hiding from its undying hunger
and it seeks, satisfaction
its stomach rumbles
and pieces of me crumble
underneath the weight of its devouring presence
absent minded of what's present before me
I miss my presence of mind
and the gifts that adored me
instead being showered with memories my brain storms me
memories in which I am unable to afford the

price of attention
left broke by the thoughts of what was once
and what's missing
I can't pay mind to what is
and is
is too busy missing you
is it true
is this my life without you
is it that pieces of me are missing
I am really incomplete without you

DETENTION

I hate to admit that I miss you

I hate to admit that

my mind is just a class

to class thoughts of you

like schools of students

school bells of you ringing in my head

needing to let you go

but I can't seem to dismiss you

you have my attention

held in detention

my emotions stuck in study hall after school

every time your name is mentioned

tattooing your name on my every thought

as if my every idea was made of chalk

and the world was just a big board

and my reward

for missing you

was to write

your name

over and over

until I could learn how to love right

because love is just about learning, *right*

the art of language

communication

spelling things out

it's about basic math

adding the sums of two different people

to equal

a greater equation

later

subtracting individualism and selfishness

then multiplying that product by prayer

but while we were together

I sucked at arithmetic and was confused by figures

my communication was subpar

you

I could never really figure out

honestly

I never really took our studies seriously

guess that's why you and I failed at love

but if love is just a school

then missing you

is just another lesson

detention must be just another way for me

to make corrections

I went through this heartache for extra credit

got my heart prepared for next semester

so yeah

I hate that I miss you

but maybe missing you

was necessary for my new direction

DEW SEASON

In the midst of it all
and in its *dew* season
all the mist has to fall
cause my miss is in its due season
for I miss you
for whatever reason,
and for whatever season
has these whatever tears bleeding
reading the blood stained signs
through the fog of it all
waiting
wanting
for this mourning to be over
so I can see again
cause quite frankly
I need to believe again
for in you
I lost hope
and found pain
a love lost
is a lesson gained
and heartache was my teacher

heartbreak was my preacher

and with him

I conversed religiously

and from the truth I was led astray

led to believe that you had to be brainwashed

or talked into

or led away

when really

you just washed away

guess I should have kept those storms away

because you proved to be so fair weather

but whether or not

the sun shines or not

I remain in the same spot

you left me in

cause the storms here we weather

we choose to be watered by the dew

cause in due season

we grow

and in due season

we learn to let go

cause in due season

we all reap what we sow

and although

the sowing of others

may at times make us weep

let us never lose sleep

cause in God's due season

we find our peace

we piece back together the pieces we lost

when others peace'd out

and left us lost

in the midst of the morning dew

for a new day is dawning

a new day here

and here is where we find our way

in God's due season

HOW DO YOU TELL

No not another sleepless night
not another night,
plagued with endless tossing and turning
has my heart spinning
my head in a daze
has regrets winning
and if love is a battlefield then
that war was waged in the minefields of my mind
and there's plenty
of damage...
it's chaotic
detonated by false missteps
mistakes have my thoughts ravished
by the explosion of the chemicals
me and you
mixed together
it's combustible
when thoughts of
me and you
are fixed together
but damn
I can't believe the war is finally over

how am I supposed to tell
the cells of my brain
that they're no longer soldiers of war
no more
do they have a purpose
no more
do they have to fight
no more
does the endless cycle of
waking up
terror
at night
but how do you tell
the cells
the soldiers of love
the protectors of thoughts
that they're an afterthought
that the war in which they fought
there was no winner
only losers
only loss
pain
how do you tell
your brain cells
your soldiers in the fight called love
that

they're going home

that

they're civilians again

that

they'll never fight again

how do you tell...

FAIRY TALES

If tears themselves could type
these ones of mine
would type a book
the type of book that would hold within its pages
pages that would tell tall tales
of once upon a time
times
the timeless memories I play of us
a book that would transcribe within its lines
lines that describe how we would stay with us
and in its words
words that write out a life where we grow old with us
it's letters themselves
would form words
the words
sentences
and in my book it would all make sense
it's just in reality
our lives together isn't fiction
see fiction hides the affliction and its addiction to pain
between its lines of unwritten truths
hidden from hearts too blind to see them

and the love-drunk minds choosing not to believe them

and even though

many grow

out of fairy tales

tears never do

they puddle up right in front of your eyes

to remind you

that you used to too

escape running down your face in search of a land far far away

where happily ever after is

leaving you a trail to follow

falling to the ground

they die in search of love...

so start your search of love

in their honor

read their pages

what do your tears type

LETTERS FROM THE WRECKAGE

We woke up fighting again this morning
and I know
I really should have called off
and worked things out with you
especially after you begged me
not to leave
but I did
and I know it seems
like I didn't care
but I do
believe me
I was so close to staying home with you
cause last night
I didn't sleep a wink
we stayed up all night fighting
things were so bad this time
you stayed up all night crying
and
I
just
went
to
bed

I just wanna let you know
I tossed and turned too
with so many thoughts
I decided to leave unsaid
I just had to clear my head
you know how big of a day
today
was for me at work
and for our future,
I just couldn't miss it
I had to come
and now look at me
trapped in a clogged stairwell
not working
can barley see
everything is so hectic
the people around me are so frantic
there is so much panic
we all are so confused
as to what happened
but all I can think about is what happened
last night
with you
but what I do know is
I heard a big boom
it was so loud
it was so rattling

it sounded as if a train derailed

I overheard Bob mentioning something about a plane

and well

I guess someone can't fly

cause with all the sky

one could use to fly by

how you hit the tallest structure around

I'm just glad it wasn't my building

imagine you are so worried

right now watching the news

you could never remember which of the two buildings

I worked in

but don't worry

I'm not in

that one

and if I didn't leave my phone

on my desk

like you always tell me not to

I could text you

and tell you I'm fine

and how sorry I am

and how I will never yell at you again

and there goes that sound again

and now the lights are out

I don't know what's wrong

but now I smell smoke

I just wanna get out

we not moving

people are starting to push

my heart is starting to rush

I hear sirens

I can't see much of anything

and it's so hot

and I just heard someone just yelled

that the other building fell

why did I have to come to work

why didn't I just stay home with you

and hold you

tell you how special you are

how lucky I am

that you are

in my life

that I never want to go a day without you

how I never want to go to sleep another night

without fixing things first with you

I don't know how long

I'm going to be stuck in here

without you

but I just wanna

tell you

how much I lo...

....

....

ECLIPSE

The shakes set in
just as the moon tucks another sunset in for the night
and occupies the dimly lit skies
by her lonesome
she is never alone...
for even though the sun's a world away
his rays makes her blush
lights her up
and all the night stars are so jealous
because she is the object of his affection
she is his one and only reflection
and during his rise
he gets a peek of her
they connect eyes
as she is on her way
to guide the hearts of the earth
for her light ignites love
over dinners
and long walks
she watches as love sparks
and he is so proud of her
he supports everything about her

and although he misses her
he dreams of the day when they can finally be together
because he is so busy being the world's light
and she is Earth's night
so timing for their love affair
never seems right
for he is committed to the day
and she's married to the night
so for now
they will have to just exist
with their love living off their morning glimpse
until she finds a way to sneak away from her night
and find his loving arms
during the next eclipse

LOVE YOU FIRST

I wanna meet a woman that makes me say
I love her *first*
not just reluctantly afterwards when she
bleeds the words
and I'm caught slowly repeating them
to avoid the most awkward of moments
stuck in a statement
that's starting to sound more and more like a question
a phrase that normally takes mere seconds to say
suddenly feels like an eternity
I'm sweating
surprised she doesn't question
my intentions
cause in those words
true feelings were clearly missing
but she quickly ignores her intuition
and hugs me to seal the deal
an embrace me for me for time suddenly feels so empty
and if guilt could kill
her innocence would be my death row
her heart chambers holding false ideas of me and her
growing old together hostage

and I have the power to stop it
to say what I said I didn't mean
but I don't wanna be labeled mean
so momentarily I spare her feelings
meanwhile
sealing her fate
sending her emotions on a crash course
and at the pace
the impact could be fatal
but every moment I wait to cut this off
her heart gains speed
and I don't have the stomach to digest the thought
of her crashing
knowing it would be my fault
haunts me
so out of obligation I stay
and I continually say
I love you?
of course only after she says it *first*
and every time I do
it makes me wish
that I met a woman
that made me say
I love you
first

LIGHTNING BUG

He called me dad for the first time
and my face lit up
the shine of a thousand lightning bugs
an amazing flash
here in an instant
gone just as fast
because part of me couldn't help
but to hear the little bit of uncertainty
jarred in his statement
as if he didn't really know whether I was
his father or merely the replacement
a stand in for his mother's boyfriend
on Wednesdays
limited holidays
and every other weekend
realizing this I couldn't breathe
my heart stopped
I should have poked holes in the top
no air
his mother just standing in there
watching this all happen
seeing my wings of joy cease flapping

she started vibrating
her man
that vulturous bird started calling
her iPhone chirping
my son was the prey
she handed my son the phone
and planted little seeds of doubt in my head
with the silly shit she would say like
you really don't have to watch him if you don't want to
this then followed by the lengthy instructions
on how to raise *my* son
mandatory I listen when he comes to see me
but this time
she fucked up
and accidently called it *babysitting*!
heaven sent tears of anger that day
danger to all around
but using my son as an umbrella
rain drops on her could not be found
she just weathered the monsoon and kept insisting
that I sat my son in front of the tube
that his favorite cartoon is the Rugrats
that he would stay glued to it for hours
that I could continue to live my life when he's with me
as if I hadn't already missed enough time
like I'm too blind to see

that he wears a faded blue shirt

with Saturn and its rings

I told her he wants to be an astronaut

that I'm perfectly capable of figuring out

my son's favorite character is Chucky my damn self

she laughed

as her inward thoughts quickly bubbled to mumbles

I overheard her say

you have no idea how to be a dad

that day volcanoes erupted

walking was disabled

because earthquakes interrupted

smoke signals and train engines were intercepted

the levees of my mind broke

my brain was flooded with questions

inception

she then planted the idea that her man

was already a better father

than I could have hoped to be

for that reason she thinks that it's best

my son calls me by my first name

for he already has her boyfriend's last

and while saying that

she said she could feel my heart breaking from all the pain

present and past

she just doesn't want the confusion to last

she says *I hope you understand*

but how could I when standing became hard

knees weak

head heavy

strong neck powered by pride needed

to keep it from hanging

because in front of my son I can't show weakness

no kryptonite

I wanna fight this

I wanna be bionic dad to him

not super stranger

but villains, will always use the people closest to you

to get to you

I know she will take my son away

if I don't agree with this

so okay I say

I introduce myself as incredible uncle

that way he'd at least know we was related

as tears began to rumble

cliffs behind teeth started to break

this unbearable heartbreak

tongues soaked into oceans

holes opened in the ozone layer

from all the stream smoking

hot flashbacks to the courtroom

still haunted by the judge's face

all stone cold and unemotional
after he dismissed my joint custody case
he played God that day
he ordered more child support
I told him money can't buy me love
I need to see my child more
but more time was out the question
he said
you get him the given time
and the rest is up to the mother's discretion
she cracked a smile,
her boyfriend rejoiced for a while
me baptized by grief
I looked up to see, a dove cried a shower
a prince...
losing his king is always supposed to be a sad occasion
unless all the Queen cares about is power
I mailed a prayer to God that day
I asked him how does he expect me to raise a child
when he doesn't grant me enough time to do so
three times bi-weekly
just won't do so
father please help me!
how can I get my son to stop calling another man dad
when he sees him three times as much as he sees me!
Mr. Metaphor are you listening

yes your honor…
case dismissed, you may leave
not without hugging my son, I won't!
I reach over to give my son a hug,
he runs and hides behind his mother's legs
points and asks *mom, who is he?*
I'm a bad dad
but honestly, that's all I'm allowed to be
I live fatherhood in flashes
here in an instant but gone just as fast

three times bi-weekly

TUMORS OF THE SEA

She told me once
that icebergs were nothing more
than drifting tumors of the sea
that instruments
if used properly
were floatation devices
that *baby, songs could be unsinkable*
the doctor said she was a cancer patient
she quickly corrected him
no! I am a singer
her notes composed of golden dust
feathers from plucked angel wings
and the essence of divinity
all good things
sweet
she sings
she was a super star
but chemotherapy and radiation
it...
it just changes things
I think she knew she was dying
the optimist
she'd make the best out of anything

she said *fuck cancer*

as she stubbornly stroked each of the malignant cords

growing inside of her organs

so loud

that even her cries sung symphonic soliloquy

her soul's piano keys playing in the back

her tearful smile shining center stage

she sang *I'm in control of things!*

all the nurses and doctors filled the aisles

and for those moments

no one cared about picking out wigs

weird prescriptions

or her depleting white blood cell count

they just stood in amazement

as I did

standing there her biggest fan

she was adorned in the beautifulest hospital gown

you could imagine

she sung

high and low

chills she gave

spotlights

had the whole unit in a daze

she hit every note

so composed

until

during her performance

cancer showed up and stole the show

she started to choke over her words

stumble

fall

I caught her

I cried for help

help!

her titanic ship was breaking

bolts busted at the seams

taking on water

loosen follicles

all of her hair fell out

she screamed so loud that day

where's the fucking doctor!?!

there he is...

what good is it to kill the bad cells

if the good ones die too!

you're not doing enough!

bae

there's got to be more you can do

bae

I'm taking my wife to a different hospital, discharge her

BAE!

WHAT?!

she said

doesn't this sound beautiful

as she played me a musical track

she knew her voice would forever be

my favorite wind instrument

she then sung all sorts of words riddled with B-flats

as the metastatic water rose to soak her toes

tickled

she just tapped her flat to faith's soggy sheet music

she grabbed my hands

and we danced

rocked back and forth

her arms cradled around my neck

my hands nestled on her backside

I

so lost her song

I didn't even notice when the water hit her knees

and when it hit her hips

she told me

baby, don't look down

as she orchestrated an elaborate orchestra

a beautiful chorus that bridged troubled hearts

and hooks of freedom

and carpe diem

just as a reminder of her beauty

and when the waters then reached her neck

she wore it like only a princess could

she made me promise
promise me that no matter what happens
that you will never forget the way that I sing
she could hardly breathe
I promise
okay
don't be mad...
but
I have decided to stop taking my medication
I asked what why?
cause that chemo shit only makes me more sick and ugly
if I'm going to die
I'm going to die being beautiful
with a head full of hair
being able to sing!
don't you love my singing?
baby, just think of my singing as swimming lessons
as long as I can still sing
my hospital bed comes equipped with motor boats of hope
music can float in oceans
believe me
I have found a way to stay alive!
not without your pills you won't
look!
you have a heart monitor
they make for horrible anchors

guitars don't get your very far
when you use them as paddles
flare guns don't come permitted with oxygen tanks
doctors don't diagnose in morse code
how won't you die?
she yelled *stop it*
I have cancer
you don't!
I am the vessel
the ship
these tumors
do not scare me
they are nothing more than icebergs
yes, I have been hit
I am going to sink
I am too sick
I know it's hurting you
but my body is the only thing about me that will die
I
we
will remain unsinkable as long as you can still hear me
baby, I cannot die in your memory
as long as you can hear me still sing
so for the few short moments I have left
let me give you something to remember me by
she started to sing another song

SPACE CADET

Captain's log day 107:

dressed in mask
gown
and gloves
the garments my cadet now refers to as my
special alien fighting space suit
are you ready for blast off cadet?
yes!
he replies
as I fasten him once again to the cold IV pump
the contraption he has come to believe is his
weaponized 8700 space modulator!
today
we continue the journey embarked on 7 months ago
with one and only one mission
combating intergalactic mutiny
so in my best
still poorly performed astronaut voice
I puff out my chest tall and proclaims
today's objective
to seek and destroy all who oppose order

to prevent this evil from spreading

throughout his universe

to capture and contain all those looking to bring ruin to it

blasters online

blasters online commander!

missiles set to fire in

3..

2..

1..

I push

the administer button on the pump

it

delivers another round of chemo

he

braces himself for the turbulence

soldiers

space driving into his atmosphere

can be overwhelming at times

it burns

he cries sometimes

his parents could never understand

the space travel thing

they think his condition is nothing to play about

but the first time I met him

I tried my best to explain

but there is just no perfect way

to tell a little boy

filled with so much promise

that he is battling an enemy

Im sure he is too young to even know how to spell

c

an

cer?

so I did what any good doctor would do

I spotted a partial rebreathing mask from across the room

placed it over my face and play

OVER

there is a disturbance we must put a stop to

OVER

we must...

what's an organ?

he interjects using the last shred of innocence

he could muster up from his 45 pound body

my parent said my organs are bad

doctor, what did they do?

I told my mom I can't help the way they act

I tried to reply

to explain

but he's now fighting a war that kindergarten

couldn't have possibly prepared him for

holding back tears

I never knew I had

trying to hold tight to professionalism

doctors

are not supposed to cry

it's against infection control code

choking

I regain character:

organs are like tiny planets

and the inhabitants of your pancreas

Mars rather

are confused

so they're attacking the other planets in your body

and it's my job to stop them

do you copy cadet?

can I join the mission

of course

but cadet

this will be the most important mission of our lives

to save your universe

from the impending doom it's destined for together

we will travel the dark skies

fight in places

most doctors and cadets are too afraid to go

the enemy grows by the day at warp speed

and Alex

you don't regenerate the way they do

but we can win
you will have to fight with everything you have
can you do this?
sir, yes sir!

captain's log entry day 301:

today
he asked me
is this what dying feels like?
after every round of radiation
he asked
is Mars fixed yet?
I'm ready to go home
back to Earth
space travel isn't fun anymore
yes I tell him
we can go home soon
but the truth is
this hospital is home now
there is no more Earth
it was destroyed three malignancies ago
and I don't know how long I can continue to lie to him
there is no hope
the galaxy is lost
I am in too deep

Houston is telling me to abort

to let go...

but I can't give up on him

they don't understand

he's no longer my patient

he is my partner

and partners don't leave partners to die alone

I gave the orders for the other doctors to go home

to be with their families

but as for me

I'm staying here tonight

and every night it takes

to fight with him until his last breath

for he is my space cadet

ready for the next round?

yes,

1.....

2....

3...

blast off

TO KILL A BLACK BOY

The red curtain of uncertainty closes
on yet another the stormy chapter of your life
but this is not the end of your story
it is merely the beginning
Hamlet still has many more lines to quote
and most tellingly
the black character cast as a little boy is yet to die
there he sits
giggling
vagueing in the distance stage left
exuberantly toying with an object that closely resembles a gun
it is not
though it is in fact a dark
mysterious
often misunderstood mass
its presence in this play
only symbolically represents the boy's innocence
in America
for he is
assumed to be dangerous and deadly
well before proper and competent examination
overworked

underpaid cop enters stage right

cue swirling pools of red and blue flashing lights

metaphors for his hot and cold temper

ironic isn't it

isn't it that

he doesn't wear his heart on his sleeve

because he never had one

instead he wears years of being bullied as a kid as a badge

when he sees black

he flashbacks to playgrounds

the orchestra plays a tune

it sounds a lot like vengeance

drums bang a lot like shots

stage lights dim a lot like eyes

that have seen this part of the story too many times

as white America learns

that it is not the toy gun in this story

that foreshadows the little boy's fate

it is being born black

in this story

that foreshadows the little boy's fate

everyone knows what happens to the black boy

death

is a far too predictable plot twist for black characters on white stages

yes

this is indeed a metaphor for injustice in this country

but this is not about that

this is not another black lives matter poem

although it does

this is a poem...

about you

the one currently on stage

who feels as if your life couldn't possibly get any worse

and about him

proof that it can..

for he is no longer breathing

and you...

well your bills are just slightly past due

and the heartbreak you suffered

was only added to your life

to bring drama to scene 2

by scene 3

it will be completely resolved

you getting married will be the climax of 4

in 5

you and your love interest will meet God

under the pearly props

he will tell you that you are forgiving

that he barely noticed that time

you stumbled over your lines

you will ask if this heaven

he will say no

that this is my heart
that you only exist inside of it
he will then leave you with a simple
yet complex proverb
you will not fully understand until act 7
he will say
live for the black boy
for you live in a world filled with too many lifeless black boys
too few breathe
too many spectators watching for entertainment
too much death
not enough celebrating life
too many actors
too many people wearing masks
unable to see
past their current character
oh child if only you open your eyes you would see
that although that red curtain closes
on yet another stormy chapter of your life
this is not the end of your story
God has much more lines to write
he is the greatest storyteller
your life is the greatest story he's ever told
so child just wait
just live
just love

just be
just breathe!
simply because you still can
and if for no other reason
do it because the little black boy
can't

FALLEN PEACEFUL

I am the fallen peaceful
the crushed pink flower stuffed in the barrel
of the rifle pointed after the blast
I am the tears of the rebel ran over
I am not an insurgent
I am a person
I am more than just the shadowy figure
seen through the riot shield
no my turban is not terrorist gear
I am only armed with signs, a fitted cap and scriptures
I am protest
knees to dirt; poor, downtrodden, the trampled and oppressed
the one handcuffed and detained
forced face down on the ground
back filled with hands and feet
no, gravel does not taste like chicken
I am not resisting,
I am just trying to breathe...
yes, my hood is on
cause I'm on the phone and it's raining
why you following me! huh?
man, I live right here...
I promise you officer

I promise you neighborhood watchman
we's promise you Ku Klux Klan that
we's innocent
see, look...
there's no gun in my hand
and no
I am not reaching for your weapon
I am only trying to reach for my life
somebody help me!
okay
okay
okay listen, I promise if you let me go...
I won't whistle at that lady again
I won't whistle at that lady again
I won't whistle at that lady again
my skin
does not mean I threw the first punch in Fruitvale station
but you are judge, jury and executioner
so I am proof
that tasers sometimes fire bullets
I am a father
I am hands up, don't shoot
I am I have a daughter
I am the gun is not real
I am my tombstone afterwards that is
I am the pain of all the impossible to find words
that mothers fish the heavens hoping to discover

to finally be able to explain to their children
where daddy went to
I am the questions, too
mom, if daddy really really really loved us
why doesn't he come home any more?
mom! what does acquitted mean?
mom, if people that do bad things go to jail
why didn't the man that hurt daddy?
I am some day my little angel will learn the truth about me
and I won't be there to protect her...
to explain
that baby sometimes juries still hang
I might be a body riddled with bullets to you
but to her I am dad
I am still poppa
so you don't understand
I can't die right now…
if I die who's gonna walk her to school in the morning?
you?
answer me!
I used to want her to grow up to be just like me
just like dad
but you changed that...
now all I want her to grow up to be…
is...
alive

REMINISCE

Thinking that those were the days

as we sit back and reminisce on

what we once was,

cause what we once was

had a hand in making

what is

so we live

with zero regrets...

though sometimes we can't help but to permit

our minds to regress

back to our recess days

and begin to ponder in the playgrounds

of our mind's what ifs

like what if

we had taken different steps

would we have left more hearts

with less footprints

or would we have taken

the same path again

if we had all of life's blueprints

or what if...

life threw more hints

would we have had as many laughs

along the way

because along that way

we found ourselves

and it was only through being lost in a forest

we only learned to put our right

foot forward

after using our left

we only learned how to walk toward

the light

only after being left in the darkness

but during the process

we left many hurt feelings in the aftermath...

so looking back on our path

we are shown the results of our actions

and actually become saddened

how could we have let

that happen

at times we live with regrets

but we have to keep *living*

with those regrets

breathe *still*

give *still*

love *still*

feel *still*

walk *still*

but remember still

that at times

it's not about how far you have traveled

but how many hearts you preserved along the way

GOODBYE FOR NOW

I got to go for a bit but
it's alright
I'm breathing
oh! look, I'm standing also
and as long as my right hand
can still write
and my left is still guarding
your heart
I will never part from you
I live in each stroke
that formed each letter
in each line
that held each word in place in each letter
I composed for you
and in the event that I don't physically make it
to the promised land with you
may each poem grab a hold of you
and your hands
during the times the journey seem too trying
to remind you that I had never left your side
that your side
I will always be by
that you are not alone...

hear my voice say those words to you

during the times

it seems you can't overcome life's obstacles

and your feet become weary

and there is barely enough life force in you to go on

hear me say

keep going

imagine the wind as my touch

see the sun part out from under the clouds

and picture my smile

embrace the valleys

let me hug you through them

pretend I'm there

that I am as real as the nature around you

believe I'm right there

telling you everything is going to be alright

let these words be my rainbow to you

gifted after a troubled storm

let the memories of me comfort you like a locket worn

let my rays keep you warm

feel the rain

as it if it was pieces of my love being pour'n

don't hide from heartache

welcome it

face it

be watered by it

for it will come for you

when it does

overcome it

don't run from it

stand tall

remember I never ran from change at all

I faced the face of it for you

trust me

it's not that scary

picture my face before you

my arms alongside yours

to help you carry

whenever the world feels just too heavy

in these words

I will never leave you

you will never have to bear any burden alone

if you need me

I am here to help you be strong

but please whatever you do

don't wait for me

don't let missing me slow you down

because in these words

I will always be around

hear my voice as you read these words

can you still imagine the sound

can you still hear what I sound like

can you close your eyes
and still picture what I smile like
can you take a deep breath
and still imagine what I smell like
I will never truly leave you
I am alive in your memory
I know it's rough
I know it's going to seem tough without me
but Ima meet you there!
I promise
before the time runs out
I'll be there
waiting for you
I promise
but in the meanwhile
I am as real as you allow me to be
I love you
hear me say it
I love you
I will come for you
hear me say it
I will come for you
don't cry
it's gonna be alright
I'm right there with you
in these words